PEARL BUCK

AMERICAN WOMEN of ACHIEVEMENT

PEARL BUCK

ANN LA FARGE

CHELSEA HOUSE PUBLISHERS

NEW YORK • PHILADELPHIA

EDITOR-IN-CHIEF: Nancy Toff
EXECUTIVE EDITOR: Remmel T. Nunn
MANAGING EDITOR: Karyn Gullen Browne
COPY CHIEF: Juliann Barbato
PICTURE EDITOR: Adrian G. Allen
ART DIRECTOR: Giannella Garrett
MANUFACTURING MANAGER: Gerald Levine

Staff for PEARL BUCK

SENIOR EDITOR: Constance Jones
COPYEDITOR: Michael Goodman
EDITORIAL ASSISTANT: Theodore Keyes
PICTURE RESEARCHER: Diane Wallis
DESIGNER: Design Oasis
PRODUCTION COORDINATOR: Joseph Romano
COVER ILLUSTRATION: Lisa Young

7   9   8   6

Library of Congress Cataloging in Publication Data

La Farge, Ann. PEARL BUCK

(American woman of achievement)
Bibliography: p.
Includes index.
Summary: A biography of the Pulitzer and Nobel Prize winner
who devoted much of her life to the welfare of needy children.
1. Buck, Pearl S. (Pearl Sydenstricker), 1892–1972—Biography—
Juvenile literature.   2. Novelists, American—20th century—Biog-
raphy—Juvenile literature. [1. Buck, Pearl S. (Pearl Sydenstricker),
1892–1972.   2. Authors, American] I. Title.   II. Series.
PS3503.U198Z698   1988   813'.52 [B] [92]   87-18234

ISBN 1-55546-645-1
    0-7910-0412-0 (pbk.)

CONTENTS

AMERICAN WOMEN of ACHIEVEMENT

Abigail Adams
women's rights advocate

Jane Addams
social worker

Louisa May Alcott
author

Marian Anderson
singer

Susan B. Anthony
woman suffragist

Ethel Barrymore
actress

Clara Barton
*founder of the American
Red Cross*

Elizabeth Blackwell
physician

Nellie Bly
journalist

Margaret Bourke-White
photographer

Pearl Buck
author

Rachel Carson
biologist and author

Mary Cassatt
artist

Agnes De Mille
choreographer

Emily Dickinson
poet

Isadora Duncan
dancer

Amelia Earhart
aviator

Mary Baker Eddy
*founder of the Christian
Science church*

Betty Friedan
feminist

Althea Gibson
tennis champion

Emma Goldman
political activist

Helen Hayes
actress

Lillian Hellman
playwright

Katharine Hepburn
actress

Karen Horney
psychoanalyst

Anne Hutchinson
religious leader

Mahalia Jackson
gospel singer

Helen Keller
humanitarian

Jeane Kirkpatrick
diplomat

Emma Lazarus
poet

Clare Boothe Luce
author and diplomat

Barbara McClintock
biologist

Margaret Mead
anthropologist

Edna St. Vincent Millay
poet

Julia Morgan
architect

Grandma Moses
painter

Louise Nevelson
sculptor

Sandra Day O'Connor
Supreme Court justice

Georgia O'Keeffe
painter

Eleanor Roosevelt
diplomat and humanitarian

Wilma Rudolph
champion athlete

Florence Sabin
medical researcher

Beverly Sills
opera singer

Gertrude Stein
author

Gloria Steinem
feminist

Harriet Beecher Stowe
author and abolitionist

Mae West
entertainer

Edith Wharton
author

Phillis Wheatley
poet

Babe Didrikson Zaharias
champion athlete

CHELSEA HOUSE PUBLISHERS

"Remember the Ladies"

M A T I N A   S .   H O R N E R

Remember the Ladies." That is what Abigail Adams wrote to her husband John, then a delegate to the Continental Congress, as the Founding Fathers met in Philadelphia to form a new nation in March of 1776. "Be more generous and favorable to them than your ancestors. Do not put such unlimited power in the hands of the Husbands. If particular care and attention is not paid to the Ladies," Abigail Adams warned, "we are determined to foment a Rebellion, and will not hold ourselves bound by any Laws in which we have no voice, or Representation."

The words of Abigail Adams, one of the earliest American advocates of women's rights, were prophetic. Because when we have not "remembered the ladies," they have, by their words and deeds, reminded us so forcefully of the omission that we cannot fail to remember them. For the history of American women is as interesting and varied as the history of our nation as a whole. American women have played an integral part in founding, settling, and building our country. Some we remember as remarkable women who—against great odds—achieved distinction in the public arena: Anne Hutchinson, who in the 17th century became a charismatic religious leader; Phillis Wheatley, an 18th-century black slave who became a poet; Susan B. Anthony, whose name is synonymous with the 19th-century women's rights movement, and who led the struggle to enfranchise women; and, in our own century, Amelia Earhart, the first woman to cross the Atlantic Ocean by air.

These extraordinary women certainly merit our admiration, but other women, "common women," many of them all but forgotten, should also be recognized for their contributions to American thought and culture. Women have been community builders; they have founded schools and formed voluntary associations to help those in need; they have assumed the major responsibility for rearing children, passing on from one generation to the next the values that keep a culture alive. These and innumerable other contributions, once ignored, are now being recognized by scholars, students, and the public. It is exciting and gratifying to realize that a part of our history that was hardly acknowledged a few generations ago is now being studied and brought to light.

In recent decades, the field of women's history has grown from obscurity to a politically controversial splinter movement to academic respectability, in many cases mainstreamed into such traditional disciplines as history, economics, and psychology. Scholars of women, both female and male, have organized research centers at such prestigious institutions as Wellesley College, Stanford University, and the University of California. Other notable centers for women's studies are the Center for the American Woman and Politics at the Eagleton Institute of Politics at Rutgers University, the Henry A. Murray Research Center for the Study of Lives, at Radcliffe College, and the Women's Research and Education Institute, the research arm of the Congressional Caucus on Women's Issues. Other scholars and public figures have established archives and libraries, such as the Schlesinger Library on the History of Women in America, at Radcliffe College, and the Sophia Smith Collection, at Smith College, to collect and preserve the written and tangible legacies of women.

From the initial donation of the Women's Rights Collection in 1943, the Schlesinger Library grew to encompass vast collections documenting the manifold accomplishments of American women. Simultaneously, the women's movement in general and the academic discipline of women's studies in particular also began with a narrow definition and gradually expanded their mandate. Early causes such as woman suffrage and social reform, abolition and organized labor were joined by newer concerns such as the history of women in business and the professions and in politics and government; the study of the family; and social issues such as health policy and education.

Women, as historian Arthur M. Schlesinger, jr., once pointed out, "have constituted the most spectacular casualty of traditional history. They have made up at least half the human race, but you could never tell that by looking at the books historians write." The new breed of historians is remedying that omission. They have written books about immigrant women and about working-class women who struggled for survival in cities and about black women who met the challenges of life in rural areas. They are telling the stories of women who, despite the barriers of tradition and economics, became lawyers and doctors and public figures.

The women's studies movement has also led scholars to question traditional interpretations of their respective disciplines. For example, the study of war has traditionally been an exercise in military and political analysis, an examination of strategies planned and executed by men. But scholars of women's history have pointed out that wars have also been periods of tremendous change and even opportunity for women, because the very absence of men on the home front enabled them to expand their educational, economic, and professional activities and to assume leadership in their homes.

The early scholars of women's history showed a unique brand of courage in choosing to investigate new subjects and take new approaches to old ones. Often, like their subjects, they endured criticism and even ostracism by their academic colleagues. But their efforts have unquestionably been worthwhile, because with the publication of each new study and book another piece of the historical patchwork is sewn into place, revealing an increasingly comprehensive picture of the role of women in our rich and varied history.

Such books on groups of women are essential, but books that focus on the lives of individuals are equally indispensable. Biographies can be inspirational, offering their readers the example of people with vision who have looked outside themselves for their goals and have often struggled against great obstacles to achieve them. Marian Anderson, for instance, had to overcome racial bigotry in order to perfect her art and perform as a concert singer. Isadora Duncan defied the rules of classical dance to find true artistic freedom. Jane Addams had to break down society's notions of the proper role for women in order to create new social institutions, notably the settlement house. All of these women had to come to terms both with themselves and with the world in which they lived. Only then could they move ahead as pioneers in their chosen callings.

Biography can inspire not only by adulation but also by realism. It helps us to see not only the qualities in others that we hope to emulate, but also, perhaps, the weaknesses that made them "human." By helping us identify with the subject on a more personal level they help us to feel that we, too, can achieve such goals. We read about Eleanor Roosevelt, for instance, who occupied a unique and seemingly enviable position as the wife of the president. Yet we can sympathize with her inner dilemma: an inherently shy woman, she had to force herself to live a most public life in order to use her position to benefit others. We may not be able to imagine ourselves having the immense poetic talent of Emily Dickinson, but from her story we can understand the challenges faced by a creative woman who was expected to fulfill many family responsibilities. And though few of us will ever reach the level of athletic accomplishment displayed by Wilma Rudolph or Babe Zaharias, we can still appreciate their spirit, their overwhelming will to excel.

A biography is a multifaceted lens. It is first of all a magnification, the intimate examination of one particular life. But at the same time, it is a wide-angle lens, informing us about the world in which the subject lived. We come away from reading about one life knowing more about the social, political, and economic fabric of the time. It is for this reason, perhaps, that the great New England essayist Ralph Waldo Emerson wrote, in 1841, "There is properly no history: only biography." And it is also why biography, and particularly women's biography, will continue to fascinate writers and readers alike.

PEARL BUCK

Pearl S. Buck, one of the 20th century's most widely read authors, devoted much of her life to humanitarian causes.

ONE

Her Finest Moment

For Pearl S. Buck—best-selling novelist, adoptive mother of nine, respected teacher, and untiring humanitarian—November 10, 1938, was a day she would never forget. As she sat at her desk, wearing her blue satin kimono and writing, the telephone rang. When she answered it, the words she heard were words no American woman had ever heard before. The voice on the other end of the line informed her that she had won the Nobel Prize for literature.

At first, Buck couldn't believe it, and said so. Within hours, her peaceful Pennsylvania farmhouse and her orderly family life were thrown into confusion. Phone calls, flowers, and telegrams came from all over the world, congratulating her for receiving the highest honor that can be paid to a writer. One reporter called to ask her to translate her first astonished re-

sponse—"I can't believe it"—into Chinese. She did, but the reporter wrote it down wrong. That night over the radio, millions of Americans heard the mispronounced and inaccurate Chinese translation. But even in mangled Chinese, the message was unmistakable—Pearl Buck had won the Nobel Prize.

Though some people felt that no woman deserved such a high honor, others praised Buck and were glad for her triumph. Novelist Sinclair Lewis, who had himself won the Nobel Prize a few years earlier, told Buck that this would be her finest hour, and he was right.

It is no small wonder that she was surprised when that telephone call came. Buck had worked long and hard to become a noteworthy writer. Throughout those long years, she had followed her own advice—the same advice she had given to her students in

In 1930 Sinclair Lewis, author of such novels as Main Street, Babbitt, *and* Arrowsmith, *became the first American to win the Nobel Prize for literature.*

China: "Know what you like best, and find a way to make a living at it." But she had never dreamed that she would win a Nobel Prize for doing what she liked best.

The child of American missionaries to China, Pearl Comfort Sydenstricker was born in the United States while her parents were on home leave. She traveled to China with them when she was only three months old and grew up there, with Chinese children to play with, a Chinese nurse to care for her, and a Chinese tutor to teach her.

For Pearl, America was a remote and unfamiliar place.

Solitary by nature and isolated as a Westerner in a foreign land, Pearl had few friends and so developed an active imagination. By the age of 8, she had decided to become a writer, but between that time and the thrilling day in Pennsylvania nearly 40 years later, she had to overcome many hardships and obstacles. During her childhood, China was torn by political strife; in the course of the Boxer Rebellion of 1900, many Western missionaries and Chinese people were murdered. Pearl's little brother died, and her mother became very ill with a tropical disease from which she would never recover.

Pearl went "home" to the United States to attend college but returned to China afterward to teach. She put in many hours of missionary work, and her heart went out to the desperately poor Chinese peasants. Their strength and kindness moved her deeply, and she immersed herself in missionary work even further, visiting Chinese homes, teaching hygiene and child care, and forming close emotional bonds with the women of China. She spent little time writing, but the seeds of her novels were being sown.

At the age of 24, Pearl Sydenstricker married a young American, Lossing Buck, who had come to China from Cornell University to teach American

After receiving word that she had won the Nobel Prize for literature, Buck told reporters, "I can't believe it."

farming techniques. Dedicated to helping the Chinese people, the young couple worked to bring Western technology of the early 20th century to the Chinese. Still there was no time for Pearl Buck to write.

Her mother's health deteriorated; her husband had a stroke. Buck gave birth to a daughter, Carol, but then learned that she could have no more children. Carol did not develop normally, and finally Buck was forced to accept the fact that her lovely little girl was retarded. She immediately adopted the first of her nine other children, a baby girl named Janice.

After the death of her mother, Buck finally began to write seriously. She wrote at night, after long days of teaching, mothering, and working with her husband. She mailed her early novels to the United States and waited months to hear replies but got only rejections. Then Buck's luck turned, and she sold her first novel, *East Wind, West Wind*. She regained her energy and her good spirits and began work on *The Good Earth*, the novel for which she would become best known. When *The Good Earth* was published in 1931, Pearl Buck became famous. She and her husband realized that their lives were taking different directions, and they agreed to divorce. Buck decided to live in the United States. She started working closely with her publisher, Richard Walsh, and soon they fell in love. Later, they married.

Pearl Buck's voice would be heard around the world. *The Good Earth* was translated into 69 languages, bringing the mysterious world of China to millions of readers all over the globe. By the time she received that thrilling telephone call in 1938, Buck had left the lonely years as an American eight-year-old in China far behind. But winning the Nobel Prize marked only the midpoint of Buck's career. This vibrant and energetic woman would live to the age of 80, write almost 100 books, and earn renown as a humanitarian.

After hanging up the phone that November morning, and once the first flush of excitement wore off, Buck and Richard Walsh began their preparations for the trip to Stockholm, Sweden, where Buck would accept the

Throughout Buck's childhood in China, the country was plagued by poverty and political strife. Buck lived there until shortly after she published her best-known work, The Good Earth, *in 1931.*

Nobel Prize. She made arrangements for the care of her children, whom she had never left for more than a day or two at a time. Accustomed to wearing simple country clothes, Buck also had to buy five evening gowns with trains for the formal ceremonies, as well as several pairs of long, white kid gloves.

They sailed on the ocean liner *Normandie* and upon their arrival prepared to meet the Swedish king. A young attaché from the Swedish embassy provided Buck with a schedule

When she accepted the Nobel Prize for literature from King Gustav of Sweden in 1938, Buck made history as the first American woman to receive this honor.

of events and coached her on etiquette and protocol. Buck practiced walking backward in a gown with a long train, for it would be improper of her to turn her back on the king after receiving her award.

When she entered the great Concert Hall for the presentation, she was sur-rounded by distinguished people and royalty. Trumpets heralded her arrival, and she took her seat to listen to the speeches that marked the occasion.

The speaker who introduced Buck praised each of Buck's books. Finally, Buck's moment came. She approached the king of Sweden, accepted her gold

Through Welcome House, one of her philanthropic organizations, Buck helped find homes for hundreds of children of mixed American and Asian parentage.

medal, citation, and check. The audience burst into applause, and Buck made her way backward to her seat.

Afterward, Buck attended a dinner for a thousand guests. Behind each guest stood a footman at attention. Buck sat next to the crown prince of Sweden, and across from her sat the king and two elderly princesses. Buck described the banquet in her autobiography:

. . . One delicious dish after another was placed before me, the *piece de resistance* being reindeer steak. Before I knew it, the meal was over! Some dishes I never tasted, for I found my plate gone before I had lifted my fork. The reason? Etiquette demands that when the King finished with a course, all plates are removed with his.

When the evening was over, Buck examined her prize and read the citation with pride: "For rich and genuine epic description of Chinese peasant life and for biographical masterpieces." The award had been given to her not only on the strength of her best-selling novel, *The Good Earth*, but for several other novels as well, and for two biographies of which she was especially proud. She had written *Fighting Angel*, about her father's work as a missionary, and *The Exile*, the story of her mother's life in China, to honor her parents. Her parents' lives had been an inspiration to Buck; now her own life of service would be an inspiration to others.

At last it was time to leave Sweden. The ocean crossing took more than a week, and to pass the time Buck wrote some verses to her oldest adopted daughter, Janice. She called them "Seasick Rhymes," and Walsh made drawings to illustrate them. One verse expressed her impatience to get home:

> The only thing 'twixt me and Sweden
> Is that the ocean is betweeden.
> I think that all the Nobel Prizes
> Should wait until the ocean dryses.

Buck received the Nobel Prize, as well as the Pulitzer Prize and many other awards, for her excellence as a writer, but in the years to follow she would become known for her work as a humanitarian. She continued to write, but she would also raise her large family, tour the world as a lecturer, and found two charitable institutions—Welcome House, an American adoption agency for children of mixed American and Asian parentage, and the Pearl S. Buck Foundation, which would educate and care for these orphans in the lands of their birth. Buck wanted to promote understanding between the East and the West and hoped to help children on both sides of the Pacific Ocean enjoy peace, democracy, religious freedom, and happiness.

Buck traveled widely during the second half of her life, speaking on behalf of these causes. At home, she and her husband practiced what she preached, adopting a houseful of children of mixed parentage and bringing them up with a genuine respect for each of the two cultures they came from.

Buck worked and lived until she was almost 81 years old, but her "most perfect single recollection," as she put it late in life, would always be of that moment when she accepted the Nobel Prize for literature from the king of Sweden.

Pearl, Absalom, Grace, and Caroline Sydenstricker sit for a portrait, with Wang Amah standing in the rear. The daughter of American missionaries to China, Pearl learned about Chinese culture from her nurse, Wang Amah.

TWO

A Child of Two Worlds

Pearl Comfort Sydenstricker was born on June 26, 1892, in Hillsboro, West Virginia. Her parents, Absalom and Caroline Sydenstricker, were home on leave from their duties as Presbyterian missionaries. Pearl was the fifth child born into her family. Two little sisters and one brother had already died in China of tropical disease, and another brother, Edgar, was 12 years old when she was born.

Pearl traveled to China when she was three months old. When she arrived in the last years of the 19th century, China was still 50 years away from becoming a communist country. China's mighty 4,000-year-old culture was in decline, and 85 percent of the population were illiterate peasants, or coolies. They lived in poverty and practiced ancient methods of farming and sanitation. Wealthy, corrupt landowners controlled the coolies' lives and profited from their labor. Other than Christian missionaries like Pearl's parents, few Westerners had seen this world. The tall, homely, intense Absalom Sydenstricker and his wife, Caroline, like other young missionaries, willingly gave up the comforts of life in the United States and traveled the 9,000 miles to China in order to preach the message of Christianity.

In September 1892, the four Sydenstrickers—Pearl, her parents, and her brother Edgar—embarked on the long

Foreign missionaries to China introduced the Chinese to Christianity and Western culture. Some Chinese greeted them warmly, but others fought to expel the "corrupting influence" from their country.

journey back to Chinkiang, China, a city on the Yangtze River near Yang-chow. Marco Polo had made the city famous when he visited it 500 years earlier.

During the first eight years of Pearl's life, her mother taught her lessons at home using American textbooks. Although Pearl lived in China, she learned about America. Each day, after a time of prayer and an American-style breakfast of porridge, Pearl's mother opened the American history book to the day's lesson. "Though we lived in China," Pearl wrote later in her autobiography, "I was taught no more of the history and geography of that land than if I had lived in Peoria, Illinois. I grew up in a double world, the small white clean Presbyterian world of my parents and the big loving merry not-too-clean Chinese world." This double world, she said, made her "mentally bifocal."

Pearl's mother was not her only educational influence. Pearl's constant companion during the early years of her childhood was her Chinese nurse, Wang Amah. Following ancient Chinese custom, Wang Amah had bound feet, which were considered desirable by Chinese men. And, like other peasant women, Wang Amah kept eggs hidden under her skirts so that the warmth of her body would help them hatch.

When Pearl was six, her brother Clyde, born a year after Pearl, died.

The Sydenstrickers sought to help China's peasants, or coolies, who made up most of the country's population. Coolies lived in poverty while the owners of the land they tilled enjoyed lives of ease and luxury.

Edgar, too old now for lessons at home, had been sent back to the United States to live with relatives, so Pearl was the only child at home. Lonely and often sad, she spent long hours reading and writing. Her first work to appear in print was a letter published in the April 5, 1899, edition of the *Christian Observer*, a religious newspaper. In the Letters to the Editor column, Pearl's words were:

I am a little girl six years old. I have a big brother in college who is coming to China to help our father tell the Chinese about Jesus. I have two little brothers in

The centuries-old practice of foot binding crippled Chinese women. Women with tiny "lotus-blossom" feet were considered more attractive brides.

heaven. Maudie went first, then Artie, then Edith, and on the tenth of last month, my little brave brother, Clyde, left us to go to our real home in heaven ...

Pearl later recalled that she found it exciting to "write something in distant China and see it not too much later in an American newspaper."

After her first success, and encouraged by her mother to write every day, Pearl became a regular contributor to the Shanghai *Mercury*, an English-language newspaper that awarded prizes for children's writing. Pearl earned pocket money by winning several of these prizes.

Pearl gained a deep respect for the ancient culture of China through her nurse Wang Amah, who took her to traditional theatrical performances like the one pictured here.

She also began to learn more about the society she lived in. Wang Amah often took Pearl to the Chinese theater and told her many stories about her own childhood. When Pearl turned seven, she began taking lessons from a Chinese tutor, Mr. Kung. A Confucian scholar, Mr. Kung instructed Pearl every afternoon on the subject of Chinese philosophy, emphasizing the teachings of Confucius. Pearl noticed that Confucius's primary principle, "What you do not like to have done to you, do not do unto others," mirrored the Christian golden rule. She was doubly determined to live by this rule.

The birth of her sister Grace in 1900 brightened Pearl's childhood, but China's economic and political problems clouded her family's happiness.

Each year Pearl read dozens of books. She read the novels of Charles Dickens, her favorite author, over and over again. Pearl's interest in helping others was reinforced by reading Dickens's novels, especially *Oliver Twist.* The author's concern for poor people and the vivid way he was able to bring them to life in his novels were an inspiration to Pearl. When she was just eight years old, Pearl decided that she, too, would become a novelist.

In 1900, Pearl's sister Grace was born. That same year, Pearl's whole life, and the life of everyone in China, changed drastically. In 1900 the Boxer Rebellion took place, and the Chinese people rose up to protest the horrible living conditions they endured under dynastic rule. Their rebellion eventually led to the fall of the last Chinese dynasty.

Throughout its history, China had been ruled by 24 dynasties: families that retained power for generations at a time. When the Chinese people tired of the abuses of one dynasty, they rebelled. Warlords fought with each other until a winner emerged to head the next dynasty as its emperor. Sometimes these power struggles lasted only a few years; sometimes they continued for a century or more.

In 1900, the Manchu T'sing dynasty, led by the aging Dowager Empress Tzu Hsi, ruled China. The empress's young nephew, Kwang-Hsu, was preparing to succeed her when Japan invaded Ko-

Tzu Hsi, dowager empress of China, plunged the country into debt during the 1894–95 war with Japan. She further weakened her dynasty through an alliance with the Boxers, who were routed by American and Japanese forces in 1900.

During the Boxer Rebellion, members of the fiercely antiforeign secret society murdered Christian missionaries and other Westerners, including this American artillery captain shown shrouded in an American flag.

Like many other Westerners in China, Pearl, her mother, and little sister fled to Shanghai while the Boxer Rebellion raged, seeking protection from American forces stationed there.

rea, a land that China had always considered its own. China failed to fight off the Japanese invaders and met defeat. The expense of war left the country deep in debt because Empress Tzu Hsi had borrowed money from Germany, France, Russia, and En-gland—money she could not repay. The Western powers began to interfere in China's affairs. "We are being carved up like a melon!" the empress was said to have cried.

Her nephew, Kwang-Hsu, could see what lay ahead. Loyal to the dynasty,

A Japanese siege gun. From 1904 to 1905, Japan fought Russia on Chinese soil for control of the debilitated country. Continuing interference by foreigners eroded the power of the Manchu T'sing dynasty while calls for a constitutional government grew louder.

he nonetheless recognized that China needed to modernize its political structure in order to become part of the new world of technology and progress. For these beliefs, which contradicted his aunt's traditional ones, the dowager empress banished him from the court. Desperate to wipe out the Western powers that she believed had enslaved China with debt, the empress allied herself with a group of ferocious thugs, a secret society known as the Boxers. The Boxers embraced a fiercely anti-Western racist ideology and claimed to have supernatural powers. They went about China killing missionaries and anyone else who wasn't Chinese—as well as many who were.

One day Pearl's father came home covered with blood. He had been tied to a post and forced to watch a Chinese convert to Christianity being tortured. He now knew that he had to find a way to protect his family and his congregation of Chinese converts from the vicious Boxers.

The danger came closer to Pearl's home every day. Missionaries evacuated to Shanghai, where the American armed forces could protect them. Pearl couldn't understand why the two worlds of her childhood were suddenly at odds and why her whole life was changing. As she wrote much later, "We were not the friendly American family we thought we had been, living in a friendly Chinese community."

An anti-Western cartoon showing Chinese beating foreigners and burning their books. Pearl's early experience as a victim of discrimination later made her an outspoken advocate of racial equality.

Pearl, her little sister Grace, and her mother finally had to leave Chinkiang and take refuge in Shanghai, leaving Absalom Sydenstricker behind. Pearl wondered why she had to leave her home, her books, and her friends just because some Chinese hated Westerners. She never forgot what it was like to be the victim of racial prejudice.

The United States and Japan, allied against the Chinese, routed the Boxers and put down the rebellion. But China was irreparably weakened, and the last dynasty collapsed.

After nearly a year as refugees in Shanghai, Pearl, Grace, and their mother returned to Chinkiang, but life was never the same again. Pearl's two worlds had been irrevocably split apart.

The Sydenstricker family decided to take another leave, their first in eight

31

years, and visit the United States. It took them one month to travel from Chinkiang to Hillsboro, West Virginia. They traveled down the Yangtze River by steamboat to Shanghai, crossed the Pacific Ocean to California on a ship, then took a train across the United States. Pearl, who had listened since babyhood to her mother's stories about the wonders of the United States, finally saw them for herself. In San Francisco, where their ship had docked, Pearl for the first time saw indoor plumbing, gaslight, cable cars, and elevators. On the trip across the country, the train stopped in Marshall, Missouri, where Pearl first tasted ice cream.

When the family finally arrived in Hillsboro, Pearl instantly recognized her grandparents' house with its vine-covered pillars: It was exactly as her mother had described it to her. She spent a happy summer playing in the fields and meadows with her cousins. One day, however, Pearl learned that President McKinley had been assassinated. Because it seemed to Pearl that the Chinese empress and the president of the United States represented the same form of government, she asked her parents, "Must we have the revolution here, too?"

Before returning to China, the Sydenstricker family spent the winter in Lexington, Virginia, where Edgar was studying at a university. Pearl attended the third grade at a small country

school there. She later remembered having learned almost nothing new in Lexington because she had already advanced so far in her own studies.

By the time her family began its long journey back to Chinkiang, Pearl had a new sense of really being an American. "When my parents took me back to China with them," she wrote later, "I went back knowing where they had come from . . . I had a country of my own, and a big white house where my kinfolk lived."

Pearl resumed her former routine in Chinkiang: lessons with her mother in the morning; Chinese philosophy with Mr. Kung in the afternoons. Widespread famine and poverty plagued China, which had been stricken by flood and drought in addition to suffering political strife. The missionaries tried to relieve some of the suffering by providing rice for the starving and by working to drain the flooded fields and keep the rivers from overflowing their banks again. China seemed a beaten nation to Pearl.

The Boxer Rebellion, the fall of the T'Sing dynasty, and the huge debts China had incurred during the war with Japan had brought the country to its knees. The Russians advanced on China, eager to gain influence in the defeated country, but Japan, which had ruled China since its defeat, resisted. The result was war between Russia and Japan. Japan defeated Russia and emerged as a world power;

Confucius (Kung-Fu-Tsu), 551–479 B.C. When the headmistress of the Jewell School discovered that Pearl placed the teachings of Confucius on a par with those of Christ, she exiled Pearl to a private room.

China remained under Japan's thumb. Noting all this, Mr. Kung explained sadly to Pearl: "It will be peaceful here in China for a while. But the storm is rising, and before it breaks you must go far away." When Mr. Kung died in 1905, Pearl was 13, and in only a few short years that storm would indeed rise. China would experience first revolution and then more war with Japan.

Without her beloved tutor, Pearl felt lost and alone. She had few companions. During 1907, the Chinese famine worsened, and Pearl's parents had no time for family life. They spent their days and nights boiling huge vats of rice to distribute to the starving Chinese. Her Chinese friends, in preparation for marriage, had had their feet bound, so they could no longer run and play, or even take long walks. Often, when Pearl walked through the streets of Chinkiang alone, Chinese bystanders hurled racial epithets at her, taunting her for having "wrong-colored" blond hair and blue eyes.

As her teenage years passed, Pearl shaped a new dream for herself: to go home to the United States and attend Wellesley College. But she was still much too young, so her parents decided to send her to boarding school in Shanghai for a year.

There was a flurry of excitement in the household as Pearl prepared to leave her family for the first time. She needed new clothes, so she and her mother studied the pages of the *Delineator*, an American magazine, for ideas. Chinese tailors then copied the American designs Pearl chose. Pearl now decided to wear her hair in a single braid with a big bow.

The Jewell School in Shanghai for daughters of missionaries was a dark, gloomy place run by strict Presbyterians from Vermont. Pearl found that she had little in common with her classmates and her teachers. Her two roommates did not share her own respect for Chinese culture. When Pearl commented to them that she found many points of similarity between the teachings of Christ and those of Confucius, the girls were shocked and repeated Pearl's opinion to the headmistress. Miss Jewell was angry at what she considered to be Pearl's heresy, and Pearl's punishment was exile to a small single room. Little did Miss Jewell know how happy Pearl was to have won this privacy. Now she could read whenever she liked and work on her first novel in secret.

Another valuable experience that the Jewell School gave Pearl was the opportunity to do community service work at the Door of Hope mission several times each week. In precommunist China, particularly during times of famine and poverty, poor people often sold their daughters into slavery to rich Chinese families. If these families were kind, they released the young women at the age of 18. But many families mistreated the girls and kept them in slavery, often forcing them into prostitution. The Door of Hope attempted to free enslaved women, train them to make a living, and find jobs for them. Pearl taught them how to sew, embroider, and knit, and offered them her friendship and compassion.

"At the Door of Hope," Pearl wrote later, "I saw the dreadful fruit of evil. Many a night I woke . . . to ponder the stories the girls told me . . . I had early to accept the fact that there are . . . men and women incurably and willfully cruel and wicked. But forced to this recognition, I retaliated spiritually by making the fierce resolution that whenever I saw evil and cruelty at work I would devote all I had to delivering the victim."

Pearl Sydenstricker's chidhood drew to a close, and she set her sights on another adventure: attending college in the United States. At the age of 16, she had determined to do two things in her life: to write novels and to help people who were oppressed. Her resolution to help the victims of cruelty would stay with her for the rest of her life as her guiding principle; her decision to become a novelist would bring her the fame and wealth that enabled her to help others in ways she never imagined she might.

While Sydenstricker attended college in the United States, traditional Chinese culture began to give way to a "new China" founded on modern concepts of society and government.

THREE

College Years

As she looked toward college, Pearl Sydenstricker decided that she wanted to attend Wellesley College in Wellesley, Massachusetts. She chose Wellesley because at that time it had the highest academic standards of any American college for women. She was determined not to go to a southern "finishing school" where the education consisted mainly of courses in home economics and other subjects meant to prepare young women for lives as wives and mothers. Her relatives were horrified by this choice: As southerners, they didn't want anyone in their family to go to a Yankee school. Mrs. Sydenstricker agreed, convinced that her daughter could receive a proper education only in the South.

There was still another reason why Wellesley was beyond young Sydenstriker's grasp even though she had been accepted: Her family simply could not afford the tuition. She finally agreed to enroll at Randolph-Macon Women's College in Lynchburg, Virginia, because the curriculum there was known to be academically rigorous.

It would be her second trip to the United States and her parents' first home leave since 1900. Because her mother suffered from seasickness, the Sydenstrickers decided to avoid the long passage across the Pacific Ocean and travel via Europe and the Atlantic Ocean instead. The trip would give Pearl and Grace Sydenstricker their

Crossing Russia by train on her way to Europe, Sydenstricker observed poverty even worse than China's. The communist ideology then gaining a foothold in Russia soon reached China.

first look at Europe and would provide the opportunity for the sisters to study French in Switzerland.

The family took a steamer up the Yangtze River to Hankow, then traveled by train to Peking, where in the distance they could see the Imperial Palace, where the exiled dowager empress still resided. From Manchuria they took a seemingly endless train trip across Russia, which Sydenstricker later remembered as "endless days of train travel across a flat wooded country, the trees of birch and pine, a weary dreary monotone." She was shocked by the conditions she observed when the train stopped at stations. "I had seen poverty in China and starvation in famine times, and I was later to see poverty in my own country, but never had I, nor have I since, seen poverty to equal that of pre-revolutionary Russia." In Moscow, she saw another element of Russian life: the contrast between the very rich and the very poor. "Even then, young as I was," she wrote in her autobiography, "I felt a fearful premonition of a world to come where many innocent would suffer because of the anger of an outraged people."

From Russia, the Sydenstrickers traveled through Poland and then to Paris and London. Sydenstricker was elated to be in England, where her favorite author, Charles Dickens, had written his novels. Her sister later wrote about their time in England, describing how it was, for Pearl, "the world in which, in her imagination, through long hours in China, she had lived many times before." Only now, it was real.

After their stay in London, the family traveled to Neuchâtel, Switzerland. They spent the summer in the peaceful

During her summer stay in Switzerland, Sydenstricker studied French and enjoyed a vacation.

Although disappointed at first by the campus and students at Randolph-Macon College for Women, Sydenstricker soon became active in college life.

Alpine countryside, then boarded the ship that would carry them across the Atlantic Ocean to the United States. Sydenstricker spent many thoughtful hours during the crossing reflecting on the things she had seen in China, Russia, and Europe. She and her father spoke often about their concerns. Sydenstricker recalled that one night he said to her, "the uprising will begin in Russia . . . it will spread to other countries of Asia, and because men of the white race have been the oppressors, all the white race must suffer."

"But Americans won't have to suffer, will they?" she asked. "We have no colonies, and we have done so much good for the Chinese people—hospitals, schools, food in famines . . . "

Her father replied in words that Sydenstricker would never forget: "The missionaries went to China without invitation. The Chinese owe us nothing. We have done the best we could, but I don't think we shall escape when the day of reckoning comes."

Sydenstricker arrived in the United States in September 1910. It was time

An excellent student popular with her classmates, Sydenstricker (standing behind obelisk) served as president of her junior class.

for college to begin, and she had to rush to get there in time. She was disappointed when, instead of the ivy-covered brick halls and wide, elm-shaded green lawns she had imagined, Randolph-Macon's new campus featured low, unattractive buildings and muddy pathways. She soon realized that her severe hairdo and her Chinese-made copies of American dresses looked dowdy and old-fashioned, and she vowed that she would not be a misfit. If this was to be her home for four years, she would make the best of it and try to fit in. With fierce determination, she began her transformation, arranging her hair in a fashionable pompadour. She then took her clothes to her brother's house nearby and created a new wardrobe by altering her dresses. She listened carefully to the speech of the southern women at the school, studied their slang, and imitated it. Years later, she wrote, "I see (those years) as an experience divided again by my separate worlds. I wanted to belong, and to belong, as I soon saw, meant that I must separate my two worlds again. I must learn to talk about the things that American girls talked about—boys and dances and sororities."

While Sydenstricker was adopting the ways of American college women, and just before her parents and sister began their long voyage back to China, Absalom Sydenstricker was invited to preach at the college. As his daughter

→ PEARL SYDENSTRICKER, A. B.
Κ Δ, AM SAM
CHINKIANG, CHINA

Philosophy

Member of Student Committee, 1911-12, 1912-13; Treasurer Class, 1912-13; Leader Student Volunteer Band, 1911-12, 1912-13, 1913-14; Treasurer Y. W. C. A., 1912-13; President Class, 1912-13; Commencement Debate, 1912-13; President of Franklin Literary Society, 1913-14; President Literary Club, 1913-14; President Senior Club, 1913-14; Senior Delegate World's Student Volunteer Conference, 1913-14.

"The Sky Pilot."

Sydenstricker participated in numerous college organizations. Though well liked, she never felt as if she really fit in, and she never forgot about China's troubles.

In 1914, the year Sydenstricker graduated from college, World War I broke out in Europe. Buck saw the war as the start of a great struggle between East and West.

sat in the chapel among the other freshmen, waiting for the speaker to arrive, she wondered nervously what sort of impression her stern father would make on her new American friends. She noticed as her father walked to the lectern that he wore his shabby, old-fashioned coat, and that his expression was severe and studious.

Someone remarked in a whisper that the speaker looked as though he'd be long-winded. After a moment, Sydenstricker admitted that the man was her father. When the other girl apologized, Sydenstricker brushed it off and laughed, saying that, in fact, her father *was* long-winded.

Sydenstricker began to enjoy the routine of college. She didn't mind the hard cots the girls slept on or that there were only three bathtubs for every 20 girls. She didn't mind the compulsory chapel service or gym classes. For Sydenstricker, all of this was part of her new American world. By the end of her freshman year, she had become a success both socially and academically, even though she still hated math and Latin.

In her sophomore year, Sydenstricker felt even more comfortable. She began to write again and won several literary prizes. She studied hard because she enjoyed her classes, but she rarely paid attention to the grades she received. Although she did not play sports, she participated eagerly in many other college activities. She spent vacations and summers with her brother Edgar and his wife and two small children, and occasionally visited the homes of her classmates. Sadly, she noticed that Americans seemed to have no curiosity about what went on in the rest of the world. Neither her college friends nor their families ever asked her about life in China.

During her junior year, Sydenstricker served as president of her class. She pledged a sorority, Kappa Delta, and joined a secret society called Am Sam. She won a short-story

prize that year and attended as a delegate a YWCA student conference at Bryn Mawr College in Pennsylvania. But at the end of her happiest college year, she received a letter from China containing the news that her beloved nurse, Wang Amah, had died. At the same time, her brother accepted a high-paying job in Washington, D.C., and asked Sydenstricker to move off the college campus for her senior year to live with his wife and help care for their two babies. She loved college life, but reluctantly, she agreed.

When Sydenstricker returned to China to teach, she found a country stricken by political upheaval and widespread famine. Tickets such as this one allowed starving Chinese to obtain meals distributed by Western charities.

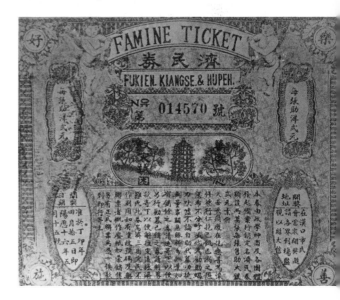

In 1912, Sun Yat-sen (pictured) had been elected provisional president of the first Republic of China, but Yuan Shih-k'ai, who had effected the abdication of the Manchus, took control of the government.

Letters from home continued to report political trouble in China. The supporters of the deposed empress and her regime were being persecuted, while a new leader, Sun Yat-sen, struggled to establish a Chinese republic. While these events worried Sydenstricker, few of her classmates shared her concern. "All that they knew about China," she wrote later in her autobiography, "was that they had heard a missionary beg for money in a church so that he could teach the Chinese or feed them or buy bibles for them, and they thought of the great and beautiful country as a land of beggars and savages." She read and reread her mother's letters and wondered if she would ever return to China.

Sydenstricker worked hard during her senior year, studying poetry and translating poems from Greek, Latin, and French. Living in her brother's house was difficult because his marriage was not a happy one. When he came home on visits she spent long hours talking with him, trying to persuade him not to divorce his wife. Despite these difficulties, she won top honors in both poetry and fiction and graduated with distinction.

Years later, she looked back on her college years and wrote, "My attempt to be like other American girls was not permanent, I fear, and after my graduation I was faced with my two worlds again. Which should I choose? Should I stay to become permanently American, or should I go home again to China?"

Sydenstricker decided that she was not ready to return to China. Thus, when invited to serve as an assistant psychology instructor at Randolph-Macon, she accepted with delight. She loved the work, though there were times of loneliness. She missed her mother, whom she worried might not be well. And she still missed China.

A letter from home convinced Sydenstricker to return to China. Her mother had contracted sprue, a fatal tropical disease that attacks the red blood cells. Her first thought was to drop everything and leave for China immediately, but it was 1914. World War I had started in Europe, and travel everywhere was restricted. Sydenstricker saw the war as a confirmation of her earlier forebodings. It was, she felt sure, the beginning of a long struggle between East and West.

Sydenstricker applied to the Presbyterian Board of Foreign Missions for a teaching job in China. When she was accepted, she found someone to take her place at Randolph-Macon and waited for an emergency travel permit. In November 1914 she sailed again for China.

On board ship, Pearl Sydenstricker received her first kiss. Sydenstricker confided later to her sister that a young American who worked for the Standard Oil Company had almost proposed. But by the time the ship reached Shanghai, she had decided that she would not see him again. She would devote herself to taking care of her mother and seeing to the education of her teenage sister. She began, as she put it, to "think again in Chinese."

When Absalom Sydenstricker met the boat, he didn't recognize his Americanized daughter. At home, the young woman barely recognized her ailing mother. The illness had taken its toll, and Mrs. Sydenstricker was thin and weak. Pearl Sydenstricker was determined to nurse her mother back to health.

Her days were very busy. Teaching brought her into contact with young Chinese men who were deeply involved in their country's political changes. She learned about China from them as they learned English from her. In addition to teaching school and caring for her mother, she also took over her mother's missionary work, counseling Chinese women.

Sydenstricker soon learned in detail about events in China since she had left in 1910. The fallen empress of the Manchu T'sing dynasty and her heir were both dead. Warlords had bickered for years over the throne while revolution was brewing. Sun Yat-sen, a doctor turned revolutionary, had emerged from the chaos as a hero. Having fought to overthrow the monarchy and establish a Chinese democracy modeled after the constitution and government of the United States,

The Sydenstrickers traveled into the mountains in bamboo sedan chairs like this one, hoping that fresh air and rest would return Caroline Sydenstricker to health.

Sun Yat-sen had become president of the first Chinese republic. But China's troubles were far from over.

Sydenstricker and her Chinese students discussed China's political situation every day in class, and the American woman grew more deeply concerned for China and its people. In years to come, her love for the Chinese would lead her into some of her greatest philanthropic endeavors.

In spite of her busy schedule, Sydenstricker often felt lonely. Once again, she did not fit in. Her Chinese friends were all married, and they often asked her when her parents would find a husband for her.

Sydenstricker began meeting and dating American men, only to be criticized by other members of the missionary community for behavior they considered scandalous. When she protested that she was not a missionary but a teacher, her critics were not satisfied. They insisted that because she lived in the mission community, she should behave like a missionary. Frustrated, she stopped dating. But she wanted to break away from this restricted life and go out on her own. A job possibility in the North opened up, but because her mother's health grew suddenly worse, she could not take the post.

As Caroline Sydenstricker's condition grew worse, the family decided that she should go to Kuling, a resort and spa located high in the mountains.

There, the air was pure and clean and free of diseases, such as the diphtheria and cholera that plagued China's lowlands. The family had spent summers there while the children were young, and they had a small stone cottage where Pearl and Caroline Sydenstricker could go. Grace Sydenstricker, attending a boarding school in Shanghai, would join them for the summer.

The journey up the mountain in bamboo sedan chairs was both more beautiful and more dangerous than Sydenstricker had remembered from her childhood. She later wrote in her autobiography:

> We seated ourselves in our chairs and four bearers carried each chair, suspended by ropes from poles across their shoulders, and thus they mounted the first flight of stone steps with light, rhythmic strides. Up the mountain we climbed . . . The road wound around the rocky folds of the cliffs, and beneath us were gorges and rushing mountain rivers and falls. Higher and higher the road crawled, twisting so abruptly that sometimes our chairs swung clear over the precipices. One misstep and a chair would have been dashed a thousand feet into the rocks and swirling waters— but there was no misstep. In all the years, I never heard of an accident.

The summer was pleasant. High in the remote mountains, the family received no news of the terrible war that was raging throughout the world. But when her sister returned to school, Pearl Sydenstricker grew lonely and restless again. Her mother seemed bet-

Although Sydenstricker was thrilled by the political and intellectual revolution taking place in China, she deplored the chaos it brought to the lives of the common people.

ter, so she left her in the little stone house and went back to Chinkiang to resume her teaching duties.

There she learned that Sun Yat-sen was no longer president of the republic. He had been ousted by a military leader who hoped to reestablish the imperial throne and install himself as the new emperor. But by now the Chinese people had discovered the advantages of self-government and rejected the idea of a new emperor. Chinese intellectuals adopted Western religious, political, and social ideals; women ceased binding their feet; education improved; and the followers of Sun Yat-sen remained intent upon building a new society.

"It was a fantastic era," Sydenstricker wrote later. "I felt sometimes as I read the newspapers that I was a juggler, trying to keep a dozen balls in the air at the same time."

One particular aspect of the changing times affected Sydenstricker in a personal way: The literary environment was changing. Literacy was on the rise, new magazines began to appear, and people clamored for novels to read. Translations of American and British books appeared in China, and thousands rushed to buy and read them. Sydenstricker's dream of writing reawakened.

After her marriage in China, Buck gave birth to a daughter, Carol, whom she later learned was mentally retarded.

FOUR

Trouble in China

John Lossing Buck, born on a farm outside Poughkeepsie, New York, graduated from Cornell Agricultural College. Deeply religious, Lossing Buck's dream was to teach modern farming methods to people in underdeveloped countries. After his graduation in 1914—the same year that Pearl Sydenstricker finished her studies at Randolph-Macon College—he applied to the Presbyterian Board of Foreign Missions for a job. He was sent to a mission station in Nanhsuchou in the north of China to help introduce American methods of cultivating wheat, the main crop in that region, to the Chinese.

One of the first trips Buck took in China was to the summer resort at Kuling, where Pearl Sydenstricker had taken her mother for the summer. The two young people met there, and Buck was invited to the Sydenstrickers' home.

It was not love at first sight, but they were attracted to one another and had similar career goals. Both had been thinking of marriage: Sydenstricker to escape the demands of her family and Buck because his salary was only $1,200 a year and marriage would bring an extra stipend for his wife. The two young people met, considered the possibility, but parted for the moment.

Sydenstricker went back to teaching and Buck to his agricultural research. They continued to correspond, and finally Buck invited Sydenstricker to Nanhsuchou for a visit. She met his colleagues and friends in the missionary community there, and they liked her.

Outgoing, intelligent, and very much at home in China, Sydenstricker fit in

John Lossing Buck hoped to bring modern agricultural technology to the peasants of China.

Although accepted quickly into her husband's community, Buck found the life of a missionary's wife somewhat confining.

well with Buck's community, but rural Nanhsuchou, unlike cosmopolitan Chinkiang, was a bleak and desolate place with few amenities. And Sydenstricker knew that if she married Lossing Buck she would be making a commitment to a lifetime of missionary work—a life that she had already decided was not for her.

When she spoke to her parents about the possibility of marrying Buck, the Sydenstrickers objected strongly. Her mother worried that Pearl would not be happy with someone who didn't seem to share the same interest in books. Convinced that Lossing Buck would learn to enjoy reading once he was under her influence, Sydenstricker brushed her parents' objections aside. She remembered, much later, that when she announced her decision to marry Buck, she heard a voice inside her that said, "This is a mistake. You will be sorry." But she went ahead with her plans.

Pearl Sydenstricker and John Lossing Buck were married on May 30, 1917, and spent their honeymoon in the Sydenstrickers' stone cottage in Kuling. Then they returned to Nanhsuchou, where they had found a small house with a lawn and a garden. Pearl Buck stepped into an unfamiliar career as a traditional wife. She made curtains, hung pictures, gardened, and even mixed red clay into yellow paint to create a restful, pleasant color for the walls of her new home. She carefully managed the tiny family budget and regularly wrote letters home to her own parents and to her husband's family in New York State. She helped her husband with his work preparing questionnaires for Chinese farmers, and when his eyes began to fail, she read to him and typed his letters.

The Chinese used ancient farming techniques, which the Bucks soon discovered were better suited to the Chinese climate than the Western methods that the Americans tried to import.

53

Buck did missionary work of her own in hopes of improving the standard of living for Chinese peasants. The opium addiction prevalent among the Chinese particularly distressed her.

Lossing tested a hundred varieties of wheat seed from all over the world, trying to find the one that would grow best in northern China, only to conclude that the type of seed the Chinese had been using for centuries was the most successful. It took him a long time to realize that what he had learned at Cornell University could not be applied in China. Finally, Pearl suggested to him that he learn more about Chinese agricultural methods before

he attempted to modernize them. He took her advice and approached his work from a new perspective. When the results of the Bucks' study were published, Buck's career as an innovative agricultural expert was launched. Meanwhile, his wife was so busy that she had little time to write.

Pearl Buck plunged into missionary work of her own, visiting Chinese women and preaching Christianity. Perhaps more importantly, she brought practical advice about child care, hygiene, and food preparation to remote Chinese villages. Her letters home began to sound less cheerful. In the barren northlands, she saw a new side of the Chinese people—one that distressed and disillusioned her. She was particularly concerned about the problems poor people faced—crime, drunkenness, and widespread opium addiction. Pearl was torn between her love for the Chinese people and her awareness that they had many human faults. Yet she continued to view the Chinese peasant woman as a heroic figure of courage and strength. These women turned to her for advice and comfort, and she felt boundless compassion for them.

Although she and her husband had a harmonious and productive working relationship and rarely quarreled, they shared no real emotional link. Lossing cared first of all for his scientific work and had no time for conversation or fun. After three years in Nanhsuchou, Lossing had earned high praise for his research and was invited to teach a course in agricultural economics at Nanking University. Pearl simultaneously discovered that she was pregnant. The Bucks moved to Nanking, and on March 20, 1918, Caroline Grace Buck—Carol—was born.

In Nanking, Lossing Buck taught at the university while Pearl Buck managed their busy household and began writing in earnest.

55

Pearl wrote to her sister Grace, in college in Tennessee, that she knew she would never tire of babies. It was a happy moment for her, but her happiness was not to last. She did not recover quickly from Carol's birth, and finally, after visiting several doctors, she learned that she must undergo surgery. In haste, the Bucks and baby Carol traveled across the world to New York, where Pearl was operated on for appendicitis and a benign tumor. She came through the operation well and recovered her strength quickly, but a terrible disappointment awaited her: She learned that she could not have any more babies.

Back in China, Pearl plunged into hard work and taking care of Carol. The Bucks settled into their new home in Nanking, and Pearl took on two teaching assignments—one teaching English literature at Nanking University, where her students came from the upper classes; the other at a government university, where they came from poor villages and had less education. Lossing, respected and successful in his career, seemed happy with his work, his family, and their attractive house and garden, but for Pearl, more troubles were in store. Her mother's health grew much worse, and it became clear that she would soon die. Grace Sydenstricker returned to China, and Buck visited her family in Chinkiang, 200 miles to the south, as often as she could. When Caroline

At the time that the Bucks lived in Nanking, Chiang Kai-shek became the leader of the Chinese Nationalist party, which for several years embraced communism. The Nationalists fought to oust the warlords who ruled northern China.

Sydenstricker finally succumbed to the disease she had been fighting for so many years, Buck brought her father, now 70 and about to retire, and her sister, 21 and very shy, into her household in Nanking.

Her life became busier than ever. She made countless guests feel at home—

A Chinese funeral procession. As the Nationalists advanced into northern China, many died in the intense fighting in the region around Nanking.

overnight guests; guests for lunch, tea, and dinner; professors; Chinese students; and friends. Longing for a place of her own where she could retreat and write, she took over a small attic room as her study. A low dormer window gave her a view out over the mountains. Here, late at night and early in the morning, she began to write the story of her mother's life. One day it would be published under the title *Exile* and would, along with several other works, help her win the Nobel Prize. Immersed in other responsibilities, though, Buck did not yet even dream of having her work pub-

When the Nationalists reached Nanking in 1927, they arrested and murdered Westerners and Chinese alike. The Bucks fled along with other Westerners who survived.

lished. But she knew that she had to write, whether she would be published or not. As she later wrote, "All those years, while my hands were busy, these novels have been making themselves in my head."

In the world beyond her attic study, huge changes were taking place in the world, especially in China. The influence of Sun Yat-sen, the former president of China's first republic, had been enormous and far-reaching, but he had lacked the power to bring democracy to China. Other forces were moving in, and gradually the country was polarized by two ideologies—one prevalent in the north and the other in the south. The northern Chinese, who wanted to bring back monarchy, still functioned under a succession of warlords, while the more progressive south supported Sun Yat-sen's new Nationalist party. But Japan's aggression during World War I and the October Revolution in Russia in 1917 brought even more change: The Chinese Nationalist party adopted communism.

After World War I, China was plagued by riots and student strikes. Chinese intellectuals in the south began to embrace communism. Students rallied to support the cause and the promise of a new China. Buck's students in Nanking were divided on this issue—those from the north favored traditional dynastic rule; the poorer students from the south supported the Nationalist party. A new leader, Chiang Kai-shek, was gaining power.

Everyone was reading, and novels were in vogue. Buck deplored the political chaos, but she loved the literary discussions it stimulated. She met poets and novelists and read their work. The old China was giving way to modern ideas and ways of life, and more people sought educations. In the midst of all this, Buck knew that she must write. Finally, with her family settled and her missionary work going well, she began her first novel. She told no one about it; she wrote in secret.

Buck's friends and acquaintances began to worry about her because she seemed depressed and preoccupied. One good friend visiting the Bucks in Nanking in 1923, noticing that Carol was not developing as a child should, discovered the reason for Buck's unhappiness. Carol was still unable to walk, and her eyes did not focus properly. Buck tried to suppress her own fears that something might be wrong with Carol, and for a while she was distracted from her concerns by her sister's marriage to an American missionary, Jesse Yaukey. But in 1924 Buck realized, after listening to a lecture by a visiting American pediatrician, that her child was not normal. She decided to take Carol to the United States for extensive testing.

Lossing had a sabbatical that year and planned to spend it earning a master's degree at Cornell, so the family set sail once more. Pearl referred to the trip as "that long journey which parents of such children know so well—seeking over the surface of the whole earth the one who can heal."

Buck consulted child psychiatrists, gland specialists, and clinics. One doctor suggested that loneliness might account for Carol's slow development. Costs mounted, but Buck sold a short story and an essay to help meet them. Finally, her search for help ended at the Mayo Clinic in Rochester, Minnesota. There, doctors discovered that Carol was retarded and would never be able to talk or walk properly. The doctors warned Buck not to let Carol dominate her life and advised that she place her daughter in an institution. Buck refused.

Buck had faced the truth, but she was not yet ready to be separated from Carol. Through the Presbyterian Mission in Ithaca, New York, she adopted

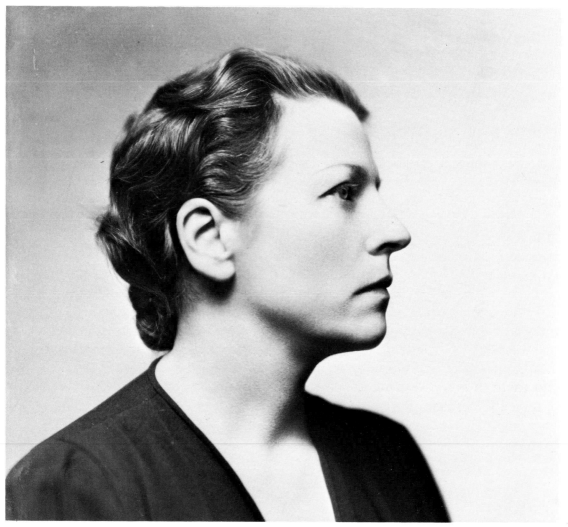

After the Nanking incident, Buck felt that her lifelong premonition of a war between East and West would soon be fulfilled.

a three-month-old girl whom she named Janice. Somehow, during this most difficult year, she also earned a master's degree. The family returned to China.

Buck turned again to her novel and continued to observe the Chinese political situation. Sun Yat-sen had died in 1925 and Chiang Kai-shek now led the Nationalist party. Enchanted with communist ideals, he wanted to subdue the northern warlords and unite China under one central government. But his relations with Soviet communists began to go sour. As the Chinese fighting moved farther into the North, closer to Soviet territory, the rift between China and the Soviet Union deepened. Fear was greatest in Nanking. Midway between north and south, Nanking was likely to become the battlefield where the opposing forces would meet. Grace Yaukey, now pregnant with her second child, moved her family in with the Bucks. American missionaries were warned to leave Nanking for fear they might be taken hostage. Many Westerners left China, but the Bucks refused to go. They strongly supported the Chinese Nationalists and wanted to show that support. They were loyal to China and regarded the Chinese as their friends.

On March 24, 1927, a Chinese friend rushed into the Bucks' home just as the family was finishing breakfast. He told them to leave Nanking as quickly as they could because the Nationalists were killing Westerners. The vice-president of Nanking University, an American, had been shot and killed. The Nanking incident was under way. Rioting, burning, looting, and killing were spreading throughout the city.

There was no place to hide. An old Chinese servant of the Bucks, who lived in a tiny mud hut in an alley near their house, saved their lives that day. She led them to her room, and there they huddled for 13 hours while the battle raged. Finally they heard shots from an American gunboat in the harbor. Help had come, and the Bucks were taken to Shanghai.

They lost everything they owned except the clothes on their backs—but they were safe. Pearl Buck did not mention to anyone her greatest loss that day: the manuscript of her nearly complete first novel.

Buck based The Good Earth, *her best-selling novel, on her own observations of Chinese peasant life. The book brought her international fame and was eventually made into a movie.*

FIVE

The Good Earth

Safe in Japan for a summer vacation and resting from the ordeal of the Nanking incident, the Buck family was unaware of the political repercussions of the uprising. Chiang Kai-shek had become thoroughly disillusioned with communism, and was in the process of breaking off all relations with the Soviets. The Nationalist soldiers who with Chiang's blessing had murdered Westerners and their friends in Nanking were now outlaws. For the moment, communism had lost its foothold in China, and there would be other trouble soon. While Chiang Kai-shek tried to eliminate communism on the one hand and vanquish the warlords on the other, Japan would take advantage of China's weakness to attack, but that was still a few years in the future.

Pearl Buck found that she could now begin to write in earnest. She started work on several stories, one of which would become, years later, the basis for the movie *The Big Wave*, about a tidal wave in Japan. Another would be called "The Revolution," and its hero, a Chinese peasant named Wang Lung, would also appear as the main character in Buck's novel *The Good Earth*.

That summer in Japan, Madame Lu, the peasant woman who had saved the Buck family in Nanking, came to the Bucks' new home. She had found out where the family had gone from Shanghai and had managed to buy a third-class railway ticket and follow them. Buck welcomed her with open arms, and Madame Lu became the family's housekeeper. When they moved to

In Shanghai, Buck participated in the city's active intellectual life and met the foremost Chinese literary figures of the day.

three-year-old Janice had an eating problem; Absalom Sydenstricker, eccentric in his old age, was demanding and fussy; and Lossing Buck required hours of his wife's time and energy every day to help with his survey of Chinese farming.

Still, Buck found time to write. She sold some stories and essays and sent one long manuscript to a New York publisher, only to have it returned, rejected, two months later. She realized that in order to get published she needed a literary agent. In an old book in the local public library, she found the names of two agents in New York and sent letters to them. One sent a response stating that people were not interested in reading about China. The other, David Lloyd, asked to see her work. She sent off a manuscript of a novel and then put the whole thing out of her mind.

Shanghai was a cosmopolitan city that had an active intellectual and cultural life. Buck mingled with an international crowd of writers and artists and was often asked to speak at their gatherings. She met the poet Hsu Tze-mo, whose nickname was "the Chinese Shelley" because he wrote in a style similar to that of the great English romantic. The two writers struck up a friendship that provided Buck with the intellectual nourishment she needed so badly and could not get from her husband. Buck later included her friend as a heroic figure in one of her novels.

Shanghai for a year, Madame Lu helped Buck run a three-family household, with Buck's family on the top floor, Grace's on the second (along with the aging Absalom Sydenstricker), and a family of boarders on the ground floor.

Buck had her hands full. Carol had become more difficult to control, and

During this year in Shanghai, Buck thrived on writing and conversation. When the family moved back to Nanking, she found that although the novel she'd been working on at the time of the Nanking incident had been lost in the looting, another manuscript, which she'd left on a high shelf, was intact. A friend had found it and kept it for her. It was the biography of her mother, written right after Caroline Sydenstricker's death. Buck now had two complete manuscripts as the fruit of her labor: one with her in China, the other on the high seas on its way to New York.

In Nanking, the Bucks again observed the chaotic Chinese political scene. Chiang Kai-shek had broken with the Communists and was bravely battling the northern warlords, but he did not appear to understand the

Most impoverished Chinese found the early promises of the Nationalists appealing. But when Chiang Kai-shek turned away from communism he began to lose the support of the peasants.

needs of the Chinese peasants. Buck felt that her earlier premonitions were being borne out and felt more strongly than ever that a revolution involving war between the East and the West was imminent. Fearing for Carol's safety in such an uncertain environment, she realized that she could not make China her daughter's permanent home. She decided to take Carol to the United States and find a safe haven for her. Leaving her first child there would be difficult, but she knew that soon she would have to move to the United States herself. "It became clear to me," she wrote later in her autobiography, "that unless I wanted to spend my life in a turmoil which I could neither prevent nor help, I would have to change my country, and with it, my world. I dreaded the change, for I deeply loved China, and her people to me were as my own."

Buck had spent more than 30 years in China, and she felt at home in her adopted land. In many ways, she felt like a stranger in her own country, but she vowed that when the time came, she would try to adopt American ways. Her decision to take Carol to America coincided with Lossing Buck's receipt of a grant to work on a project at Cornell University for the U.S. Department of Agriculture. The family sailed again, for America.

Buck's first priority upon arriving in the United States was to find a place for Carol. She visited many institutions but couldn't seem to find one that had the calm, caring atmosphere she sought for her child. Finally, after a long search, she discovered the Vineland Training School in New Jersey. It was everything she wanted for Carol, but fees were $1,000 a year—a huge sum of money in the 1930s. Buck applied to the Presbyterian Foreign Mission Board for a loan and took on a writing project for them in order to help pay Carol's tuition. Her work produced *The Young Revolutionist*, a book for children that explained the role of missionaries.

No sooner had she started writing than a cable arrived. The cable, from David Lloyd in New York, had followed her all the way from China, and its contents would change Buck's life. It contained the news that the John Day Company, the 29th publisher to whom Lloyd had sent Buck's manuscript, had decided to publish it. Buck later described how she felt when she received the cable: "The news came on a morning when I was feeling very desolate at the prospect of a future separation from my child, and while it did not compensate, nevertheless it did brighten my life in its own way." Though not ecstatic about the imminent publication of her work, Buck was pleased that she could now pay back the Mission Board loan and cover Carol's expenses for several years.

Buck's first novel told the story of a Chinese woman who entered marriage anticipating a happy life filled with love but who slowly realized that hers would in fact be an empty, lonely experience. Richard Walsh, the president of John Day Company, who would be Buck's publisher throughout her entire career, wanted to change the title of the novel from *Winds of Heaven* to *East Wind, West Wind*. Buck agreed, signed her contract, and soon became a published writer.

Buck returned once more to China with her husband and Janice and took up writing on a full-time basis. Relieved of the responsibility of caring for Carol, she had more time to herself. She

Buck's first novels told of the hardships faced by Chinese peasants. In The Good Earth, *a typical rural farmer named Wang Lung flees famine to work in the city.*

Communist leader Mao Tse-Tung (right) started to gain power in the countryside by the 1930s. After driving Chiang Kai-shek into exile in Taiwan, Mao would become the first leader of the People's Republic of China in 1949.

finished *The Young Revolutionist* and wrote a short novel, *The Mother*, about the life of a Chinese peasant woman. Buck based her story on the experiences of Madame Lu. Then, typing with two fingers, as she would all her life, she started work on what would be her most successful novel. She called it *Wang Lung*, for the Chinese peasant who was its main character.

Wang Lung's story was a tale of the earth. He and his wife tilled the land and raised children, living in poverty but getting by until a terrible famine caused them to flee their home in the north of China and make their way to the south. There, by backbreaking labor as a ricksha puller, Wang Lung managed to keep his family from starving. Eventually he grew rich and was able to send his sons to school. As educated sons of a wealthy man, growing up in modern China, they had no interest in farming. At the end of his life, Wang Lung had plenty of possessions and led a life of leisure, but he was not a happy man. He yearned for the farming work he had done in his youth—he yearned for the good earth.

When Richard Walsh received the manuscript, he read it and immediately suggested a new title for it: *The Good Earth*. Again, Buck agreed to his suggestion. "You have written a book of permanent importance," Walsh wrote to her, "one that will rank with the great novels of the soil."

Buck was elated, though still preoccupied with the worsening political

China's ongoing war with Japan prevented the Nationalists from establishing a stable government. As the situation in China grew more threatening, Buck took her daughter Carol to safety in the United States.

scene in China. A young leader had arrived on the scene to bring renewed strength to the Communist party. His name was Mao Tse-tung. Meanwhile, Chiang Kai-shek's power was waning.

But good news arrived from the United States: the Book-of-the-Month Club had selected *The Good Earth*, which would probably help the book sell many additional copies. When the book was published in 1931, it was a success with the critics, and soon the John Day Company had sold 40,000 copies. Richard Walsh submitted the novel as a candidate for the Pulitzer Prize.

Then, just as Buck was completing her next novel, *Sons*, the Yangtze River overflowed its banks and a terrible flood ensued. Twenty-five million lives were lost in this flood. Buck donated money she made by selling stories and articles in China to a flood relief fund.

American aviator Charles Lindbergh and his wife, Anne Morrow, flew over China in their airplane, surveying the damage and spotting isolated villages where rescues could be made. They saved thousands of lives, but just as they took off to return to the United States, something went wrong. While thousands of Chinese spectators watched, their plane plunged into the Yangtze River. The onlookers believed that the river god had taken the foreigners but were astonished when the aviators climbed out of the wreck unhurt.

When the Yangtze River flooded in 1931, 25 million Chinese lost their lives.

While Buck's novel triumphed and China suffered, Absalom Sydenstricker died. The flood prevented Buck from reaching her father's bedside before he passed away, and her grief was enormous, for she had loved him greatly.

Soon, Buck had another problem: The missionaries among whom she lived and worked condemned her for the honest portrayal of the sexual life of the Chinese peasant in *The Good Earth*. The Presbyterian Foreign Mission Board accused her of "unmentionable depravity." At the same time, American reviewers praised the book highly for its frankness, and movie producers clamored for the rights to make a film of the story.

Busier than ever, Buck hired a personal secretary and began making speeches and appearances in Nanking. Will Rogers, the popular American movie star and columnist, came to China to meet her. He then wrote his first book review—a glowing recommendation of *The Good Earth*. Hundreds of thousands of Americans rushed out to buy the book. Buck's publishers told her about the storm of publicity her book was generating in the United States and asked her when she was coming back. Buck accepted $50,000 from Metro-Goldwyn-Mayer for the movie rights to *The Good Earth*. The Theatre Guild bought the dramatic rights and commissioned a play to be written. Then she learned that she had won the Pulitzer Prize.

Aviator Charles Lindbergh and his wife, Anne Morrow, flew over the flooded region around the Yangtze River and helped save thousands of lives.

Lossing Buck decided to go back to Cornell for a Ph.D., so the Buck family traveled once more to America. Richard Walsh tried to shield Buck from the press, whom she dreaded, but after her first few encounters, the new celebrity found that she enjoyed the limelight.

The Good Earth sold almost 2 million copies in 1931 alone. Everyone was

When Will Rogers reviewed The Good Earth, *sales of the book skyrocketed.*

Criticized by the Presbyterian Foreign Mission Board for her straightforward depiction of sexuality in The Good Earth, *Buck eventually resigned her missionary post.*

reading and talking about *The Good Earth*, and everyone wanted to meet its author. Since then no other American novel, except perhaps *Gone with the Wind*, has ever been so popular.

After a quick visit to Carol, who was content in her school, Buck embarked on a whirlwind publicity tour filled with lunches, teas, dinners, and speaking engagements. She traveled throughout the United States and was received warmly everywhere. With the money she earned by writing, she created a permanent trust fund for Carol, endowed the Vineland Training School, and had a special home, The Carol Cottage, built for Carol and her fellow students. She wanted her child's life to have meaning and be filled with pleasure, and the Carol Cottage was built to provide every comfort to its residents, including a swimming pool and a playground. Buck also contributed funds toward research in the field of preventing mental retardation. That research continues today.

At Yale University, Buck received an honorary master of arts degree; at Randolph-Macon, her alma mater, she gave a commencement speech and enjoyed a reunion with her classmates. The very height of her publicity festivities, however, was a gala dinner at the Waldorf-Astoria Hotel in New York. All of literary New York turned out to meet the new author and Pulitzer Prize winner. The dinner, with 200 guests, was

Buck received many awards for The Good Earth, *including an honorary degree from Yale University.*

reported in all the newspapers. Then the famous radio commentator, Lowell Thomas, praised the book on his nightly news broadcast, and thousands more copies were sold.

Buck began to enjoy her new fame and wealth, and the respect she had won as a novelist.

Buck used her name and influence to raise funds for a variety of causes, including assistance for Chinese children orphaned during the Sino-Japanese War (1937–1945).

SIX

A New Life in America

Pearl Buck was on top of the world. People stopped on the street and asked for her autograph, her name was always in the papers, and her phone rang constantly. Throughout it all, Richard Walsh was by her side.

The stage version of *The Good Earth*, with Sidney Greenstreet in the cast and Claude Rains in the role of Wang Lung, opened on Broadway. It was only modestly successful, but the novel's sequel—*Sons*—was published at the same time and was a critically acclaimed success. In *Sons*, Buck depicted the urban world of the new China. Wang Lung's sons, educated and involved in politics, were the heroes of her new novel.

Buck's many speaking engagements included an evening in Harlem in New York City, where she spoke to a group of black women. This meeting gave her a new awareness of the racial tensions that troubled the United States, and Buck decided that when she came to live in this country permanently she would make racism her first concern.

She returned to China with her husband, who had earned his Ph.D. and was eager to get back to his work. In China, Buck told her husband that she wanted a divorce, and he reluctantly agreed. Their marriage ended without rancor: Each simply realized that their lives were moving in different directions. Pearl Buck returned to the United States to stay.

Buck's publishers were impatient for another novel, but the dramatic changes in her life made writing diffi-

Buck enjoyed the fame that accompanied the success of her novel The Good Earth. *Here she receives an award from the American Academy of Arts and Letters.*

cult for her. Then she remembered the manuscript that had been saved during the Nanking incident. *The Exile*, Buck's biography of her mother, came out of hiding and was published to great popular and critical acclaim. Meanwhile, Buck went to work as an editor at the John Day Company. She completed *House Divided*, the third novel in what would be called "the good earth trilogy." The story of Wang Lung's grandsons, *House Divided* tells the tale of a Chinese student, educated in the West, who is torn between two worlds—traditional China and the modern West. *The Good Earth*, *Sons*, and *House Divided* together tell the story of the tumultuous first half of the 20th century in China.

Pearl Buck and Richard Walsh soon realized that they had fallen in love. Though at first worried that a second marriage might cause a scandal, Buck finally listened to her heart. She and Walsh were married in a simple ceremony in Reno, Nevada.

Eager to put down roots, Buck began searching for a country home and soon bought a charming old stone farmhouse with 50 acres of land in Bucks County, Pennsylvania. She went back to her desk right away to write another book, a companion volume to the biography of her mother. *Fighting Angel*, the story of her father's life as a missionary, was also a success. The Book-of-the-Month Club featured *The Exile* and *Fighting Angel* as a dual offering. The reviews of those works were excellent, but Buck decided that she would not write any more biographies. She found the form confining and preferred to write novels. In an article in the *Chicago Tribune*, she wrote, "The difference between the writing of fiction and biography is the difference between being free to roam the hills and having to walk within a walled garden. Fiction is painting; biography is a photograph. Fiction is creation; biography is arrangement. For the creative writer, biography is far more difficult ... I do not think I shall ever write other biographies. I like the freedom of creative writing. I like choosing and making my own characters. But I am glad to have put into some sort of permanence, nevertheless, these two beloved characters of my life."

Buck and her new husband lived and worked in New York City during the week, in a penthouse apartment with gardens and terraces. They spent their weekends in the country, remodeling their house, adding gardens and barns, building a swimming pool, and enjoying the outdoors. Janice, now 10 years old, went to school in New York and spent weekends in the country with her family. But the big house in Pennsylvania seemed empty with only one child. Both Walsh and Buck had always dreamed of having a large family, and they decided that now was the time. Never one to do things halfheartedly, Buck made arrangements to adopt two newborn babies. Richard and John joined the family when they were only 10 days old. Buck and Walsh transported the babies from New York to Pennsylvania and back every weekend in big laundry baskets, stopping at

Soon after her divorce from her first husband, Buck married Richard Walsh, her publisher.

Seeking a home for her growing family, Buck bought this farmhouse in Pennsylvania. It served as a welcome retreat from her busy life as a public figure.

a Howard Johnson's on the way to have their bottles warmed.

Buck gradually stopped working as an editor and spent more and more time writing. By now she was at work on her first "American" novel. She had noticed, in her first years in the United States, that women had a hard time entering male-dominated professions. She believed that women should go out and work; that they should be independent and not confined to staying home and taking care of their husbands and children. At the same time, she realized how hard it was for women to overcome traditional restrictions on their freedom to pursue their own goals. Buck especially noticed how hard it was for women artists to practice their profession while being expected to satisfy a family's daily demands. It was this conflict that she dramatized in her next novel, *This Proud Heart*. It tells the story of a talented and creative woman sculptor's struggle to fulfill her conventional role while practicing her art. This novel reflected Buck's own life, for though she was happily married to Richard Walsh and loved her home and her adopted children, she always felt that the creative side of herself existed alone and unsupported.

This Proud Heart was not a critical success. Reviewers considered it a "soap opera," but women all over the country loved the book. Buck was flooded with mail from her readers. She had become a spokesperson for the women of her country.

She began writing articles and stories for women's magazines and was criticized for writing for a popular rather than a literary audience. She responded with outrage: "One cannot dismiss lightly," she wrote, "a magazine bought and read by three million people." No matter what the critics said, Buck was determined, whether writing about China or about the women of America, to promote understanding between people and to try to achieve justice for all. She was determined to reach a broad audience; she wanted to be read by everyone, even by people who didn't usually read books. She was proud to speak directly to millions of American women and to help those women improve their lives. But there was another reason, too, why

Deeply concerned with improving women's lives, Buck (left) lent her name to a number of feminist causes. She supported the efforts of birth control advocates Margaret Sanger (center), and Katharine Houghton Hepburn (right), mother of the noted actress.

Pearl Buck wrote so prolifically: She needed money. As Green Hills Farm, her home in Pennsylvania, grew with the addition of buildings, animals, and furnishings, she needed more money. She and her husband had also adopted two more babies: a boy named Edgar and a girl named Jean, and the cost of household help was daunting.

Nineteen thirty-seven was a hard year for Pearl Buck. Her sister Grace, who was still in China with her missionary husband, had difficulty giving birth to her third child. The baby,

Anne, suffered severe neurological damage at birth, and it was feared that she would be permanently paralyzed. Buck insisted that her sister bring the baby to the United States for treatment. They searched for a cure, but to no avail. Anne eventually died when she was three years old. Then Pearl's only brother, who lived nearby in Pennsylvania and suffered from a heart condition, died suddenly.

In addition, the movie version of *The Good Earth* was finally released in 1937, but it was a limited triumph. The movie, it seemed, had been jinxed from the beginning. When the film company had arrived in China to shoot the movie, they had encountered resistance from the Chinese Nationalists, who objected to the portrayal of the poverty of the Chinese peasant. The Nationalists tried to convince the film

As the winner of the 1938 Nobel Prize for literature, Buck (front row, second from right) was the second woman to receive that honor. Sigrid Undset (front row, center) was the first.

The years of World War II were the most prolific of Buck's literary career. In 7 years, she wrote 10 novels and scores of shorter pieces.

America based some of its aerial fighting squadrons in China during World War II. These forces fought the Japanese for control of the Pacific region.

company to sweep the streets of the villages before filming and to dress the peasants in freshly ironed clothes and put flowers in their hair. When the company refused to use a tractor instead of a water buffalo for plowing the fields, sabotage took place: When the movie crew returned to the United

States, they discovered that all the film had been contaminated by acid. In the end, most of the movie had to be filmed in the United States.

Then, in 1938, the greatest honor of Buck's life came to her: She won the Nobel Prize for literature. The first American woman to be so honored, Buck reflected once more on the difficulty of being a woman artist. She wrote later, "The experience of receiving the Nobel Prize focused and put into sharp clear example the difficulty of a woman's sharing her total life, even with the man she loved. I couldn't do it. . . . It doesn't matter how much a woman loves a man and responds to and respects him, and no matter how

Buck's East and West Association sought to promote understanding between the peoples of Europe and North America and those of Asia.

indispensable he is, there are parts of life that cannot be shared."

As she prepared to go to Sweden to accept the Nobel Prize, she thought about America's position in the world and of the struggle between East and West that had worried her for so long. She wanted to explain, in her acceptance speech, how close she felt both to America and to China and how closely linked those two countries were. At the ceremony she said, "The minds of my own country and of China, my foster country, are alike in many ways but above all, alike in our common love of freedom. And today, more than ever, this is true, now when China's whole being is engaged in the greatest of all struggles—the struggle for freedom."

When the festivities in Stockholm were over, Buck was happy to board the ship to go back home. Grace's fourth child had been born the day

Among its other activities, the East and West Association sponsored shortwave Chinese-language broadcasts from America to China.

before Buck had sailed to Sweden, and she was eager to see her. But above all, she longed to see her own children again. She had said to Grace, before leaving, "I wish I were having the baby instead of the Nobel Prize." On board ship she wrote her "Seasick Rhymes for Janice," including this final verse:

> Higgledy piggledly
> Steamers are wiggledy.
> Flibberty, gibberty
> Statue of Liberty.

Winning the Nobel Prize gave Buck a huge boost of confidence; she couldn't wait to start writing again. The years between 1939 and 1945, when World War II raged, were among her most productive. She wrote 10 novels and many essays, articles, children's books, and speeches. She spoke and lectured widely about racial equality; she spoke about the role of women; and she spoke about the political turbulence in China, where the communists were

Eleanor Roosevelt (second from left) shared many of Buck's humanitarian goals.

gaining ground. Japan attacked China and Hitler invaded Poland, and the world's attention shifted to the war in Europe. England and France declared war on Germany. Then, on December 7, 1941, the Japanese bombed Pearl Harbor. During the war years, Buck continued to worry that the world would become polarized between Westerners and Asians; specifically that China, Japan, and India might form an alliance and try to defeat the Western powers. But nobody listened, and civil war continued in China.

In an effort to improve relations between East and West, Pearl Buck founded the East and West Association. She spoke with Eleanor Roosevelt about international problems and frequently gave radio broadcasts. As her thoughts focused on the war in the Far East, her writing, too, returned to Chinese themes. Her next novel, *Dragon Seed*, was another story of Chinese peasant life. Though she felt that "war is dull," she remarked that "I shall write one more book . . . out of a sort of duty to China and what the Chinese are now enduring." *Dragon Seed*, a story about Chinese suffering under Japanese rule, was an immediate success. It was published just as Japan invaded China, and its closing words rang in the world's ears that terrible year: "The ordeal of the conquered peoples will be heard. We must give them the conviction that their suffering and their resistances will not be in vain. The tunnel may be dark and long, but at the end there is light."

Buck worked hard for the China War Relief, raising money to help Chinese refugees. She labored to convince Americans not to hate the Japanese after Pearl Harbor, to no avail. She continued to press for understanding between East and West, but during World War II few Americans felt sympathy for any Oriental people: They were the enemy. Still, Buck spoke out: "The only kind of world fit for human beings is a world where everybody is born free." But the hour for her words was not right, and she was not heard.

Back in Pennsylvania, Green Hills Farm was a pleasant retreat from the war-torn world. When not at her desk writing her obligatory 2,500 words a day, Buck cared for her 5 children, supervised the farm activities of cows, pigs, ponies, and throngs of dogs and cats, worked in her victory garden, and canned and bottled fruits and vegetables to feed her family all year round. Her blond hair was streaked with gray now, but her energy never flagged. Each morning she worked on her next novel, *The Promise*, and each evening there were games and stories with her children. She wrote in her diary, "I have everything for happiness and am very happy, and yet, in the night, or a dozen times a day, I find myself thinking furiously about the peoples of the world, as if they were my personal responsibility."

During the last 30 years of her life Buck (right) devoted the greater portion of her time to helping children of mixed Asian and American descent.

SEVEN

The Big Wave

Pearl Buck now took little time for herself and found few hours for relaxation. Yet as she grew older she learned to appreciate the small joys of daily living, which she found could provide comfort in the face of tragedy and joy despite the terrible struggles that plagued the world. Those struggles concerned her now more than ever, and she hoped to help right the wrongs of the world. In particular, Buck was drawn to fight for the rights of abandoned children everywhere.

Between the end of World War II in 1945 and the end of her career almost 30 years later, she continued to write novels, children's books, essays, and magazine articles, but during this period of her life, writing was her second career rather than her first. Her prime concern now was philanthropy. Gradually, as the years went by, those two careers merged into one as her writing more clearly reflected her political beliefs. Frustrated because her American readers continued to think of her as a writer only about China, and eager to express her ideas about America and to write novels with American themes, Buck adopted a pseudonym. Using the

Because of her interest in improving relations between the United States and communist China, Buck erroneously appeared on the list of Red Sympathizers devised by Senator Joseph McCarthy (shown at right) in the 1950s.

name John Sedges, she wrote three novels between 1949 and 1953; *The Townsman* was the most successful of the three. During these years, she also wrote three novels under her own name; *Pavilion of Women* was the most famous of these.

In the decade following World War II, Buck spoke passionately in public about foreign policy and about Ameri-

ca's relationship with China. In 1949, the People's Republic of China was established, with Mao Tse-tung as its ruler. Chiang Kai-shek fled to Taiwan and Communist China turned its back on the Western world. Alarmed, Buck urged that the United States keep the channels open to the Chinese people by maintaining trade ties and friendly relations with China. "Our only hope,"

Asked for help by other parents of mentally handicapped children, Buck funded research into mental retardation. She is pictured here proposing that Ellis Island, the former immigration station, be converted for use as a diagnostic center for the mentally retarded.

she said, "is that Russia will show her evil side to China." Despite the fact that Buck spoke eloquently and clearly against communism, her name was added to Senator Joseph McCarthy's infamous list of so-called red sympathizers, along with those of Charlie Chaplin, Danny Kaye, Frank Sinatra, and many others. Buck insisted that she was "anti-Communist to the last drop of my blood," but at the time the accusation hurt her career: Many speaking engagements were canceled and magazines were hesitant to accept her work.

The Red Scare finally ended in the late 1950s and Buck's name was cleared. She kept busy raising her family, visiting Carol at the Vineland Training School, writing, and enjoying life in

Buck and her husband Richard Walsh adopted nine Amerasian children.

and how difficult it was for them. She was reminded of how President Franklin Delano Roosevelt, himself crippled by polio, had helped people to accept and understand physically handicapped people. She decided to do the same for retarded people. She wrote an article, "The Child Who Never Grew," for the *Ladies' Home Journal*. Mail poured into her home, and the article was soon published as a book.

Buck then turned her attention to the plight of homeless Asian children. She learned of a child born to an American missionary and an East Indian whose case no adoption agency would accept. Buck and her husband adopted the child, and soon afterward they adopted another whose parents were a Chinese surgeon and an American nurse. "I was indignant," Buck wrote later, "so I started my own agency." With seven children of her own at home, she realized that she could not continue to adopt children into her own family indefinitely. She founded Welcome House, Inc., an adoption agency for children of mixed American and Asian blood, with the aid of a board of directors that included Oscar Hammerstein. The first Welcome House Cottage, near her home in Pennsylvania, housed nine Amerasian children. Buck wrote another article for the *Ladies' Home Journal* and was once more flooded with mail from adoption agencies as

the country. Aware that she had a retarded daughter, parents of other retarded children began to seek her advice. And Buck learned of the shame many parents of retarded children felt

One of Buck's adopted children, Chieko Usuki, was born in Japan and became a U.S. citizen in 1962, at the age of 13.

Welcome House placed hundreds of Amerasian children with adoptive American parents, but because immigration laws barred many from the U.S., Buck decided to form an organization that would help these children in their countries of origin.

well as from parents who wanted to adopt babies. But adoption laws were very strict at the time: Agencies were required to match babies to their adoptive parents according to religion, skin color, even the color of their eyes and hair. Buck and Welcome House worked hard to liberalize these laws so that Amerasian children could find homes despite their racial background.

Because Buck suffered terribly in the summer months from hay fever, she bought a large plot of land in Vermont. Buck, Walsh, and their children camped there during the summer, cooking over an open fire and sleeping under the stars. Buck wrote her autobiography, *My Several Worlds*, published in 1953, and it met with tremendous success. Everyone wanted to read about Pearl Buck's life.

That same year, Buck and her family took a cross-country trip by automobile so that her children could learn about the United States. But Richard Walsh had a stroke during the trip, and it had to be cut short. Because Walsh never regained his strength, Buck would have to manage her family, her literary affairs, and her humanitarian work alone.

Now that Welcome House was prospering, Buck turned her attention to the thousands of abandoned children fathered by American soldiers in Japan, Korea, and other Asian countries. Another author, James Michener, also became aware of this problem on a trip to Asia and wrote about these children, bringing them to the attention of Americans. Buck wanted to find a way to bring Amerasian children to the United States, but strict immigration laws prevented it. She began to lay the groundwork for a way to bring help to them in their own countries.

Meanwhile, she learned of an abandoned child in Germany whose father was a black American soldier. Despite Buck's age—she was 59—and her husband's failing health, she took 5-year-old Henriette into her family. Later she adopted Johanna. Busy as she was with her growing family and her work, Buck felt lonely and started looking for a new project. She wrote two more novels, *Come My Beloved* and *Imperial Woman*, but she yearned for something new. She tried her hand at writing plays and wrote for radio and television, then a brand new medium.

Then she met a young movie producer and director, Ted Danielewski, who wanted to make a movie out of a children's book she had written several years earlier. Based on the events following a disastrous tidal wave in Japan, the book, *The Big Wave*, had already been filmed for TV. Danielewski teamed up with a Japanese film company and invited Buck to accompany him to Japan to make the movie. At first, she was reluctant to go. Her husband's health had deteriorated

Buck joined the movie crew at the filming of The Big Wave, *a children's story, on location in a Japanese fishing village.*

sharply, and the children were still young. But the pull of adventure was strong. She embarked for Japan.

The filming of *The Big Wave* was a major undertaking. An entire fishing village in Japan was involved in the shooting, with the residents playing small parts. Some of the scenes involved the fishermen going about their daily work. But the weather continually interfered with the shooting schedule, and the crew and villagers grew frustrated during the long delays. Buck later described the experience in a book called *A Bridge for Passing*. She tells of a day when, after the rain had finally stopped and the filming could begin, a cameraman fell into a rice paddy and broke his arm. Then, as the crew filmed a barnyard scene, the duck they had hoped to use turned out to be huge, instead of the small pet duck the script called for. A dog was also part of the action, and instead of playing quietly, it chased the chickens and caused complete mayhem on the set. The next day, when a rainy scene was scheduled to be filmed, the sun came out, and the crew had to fake the rain. Buck wrote, "The men climbed on the farmhouse roof and rigged up the best rainmaking machine in the world, namely, a hollow bamboo pierced with holes with a rubber hose attached to one end. A beautiful flow of fake rain dripped over the eaves and down into the lake of mud made—in past days— by the *real* rain."

Buck loved the scenes of fishermen carrying their nets to their boats and setting out for a day's fishing. Crowds of people watched as the crew filmed the departing boats putting out to sea in a long row. The movie crew moved on to a new location, the village of Kitsu, located in the hills. There, the sun was shining, but alas, the script called for rain. Again, the crew had to set up their rainmaking apparatus. "We made rain all day and all night," Pearl Buck wrote, "until we pumped the village well dry. Each time we were ready for the scene, someone shouted that the water had given out, and our pump went to work again. Then, just as we were ready for the scene, actors in position and rain pouring, the makeup man discovered a hair out of place on the star's forehead, or a rill of sweat on his brow, and by the time that damage was mended, once more we had no more water, and so no more rain."

Finally, in spite of the difficulties, the film was nearly finished. The actual tidal-wave scene—all done in miniature—was filmed in a special-effects studio in Tokyo. Pearl Buck described the scene later: "They had reconstructed the village of Kitsu, with the houses three feet high, each in perfect miniature, and everything else in proportion. A river ran outside the studio, and the gushing water for the tidal wave would be released in the studio by great sluices along one side."

Though she enjoyed the experience of shooting a movie and felt a tremendous sense of accomplishment upon ending the project, Buck was grief-stricken when she received word that her husband had died in her absence.

The filming of those last few scenes was tense. The scene had to be shot over and over again, but at last the picture was complete. The happiness of their success, however, was short-lived. Buck received a cable from the United States that bore the message that her husband was dead. She took the next plane home.

Buck retreated into private reflection in an attempt to overcome her grief. Her sadness was eased by her lifelong ability to rely on herself, and her mind turned toward life. She put her personal philosophy into words and shared it in a letter with one of her adopted daughters, Jean, a student of music. "The self-discipline necessary for making beautiful music is the discipline an author needs to write great books, an artist to paint great pictures, a surgeon to perform an operation, a scientist to make a discovery. For that matter, the same discipline is essential for any great accomplishment in life.

And the greatest satisfaction comes not from without, but from within. The greatest rewards come not from the discipline applied by others—your teachers or your parents—but from the most beautiful and severe of all disciplines, that which you exert on yourself." Buck went on to add words that could stand as an epigraph for her life: "The uncommitted life is not worth living; we either believe in something, or we don't."

This time of loss was a time of assessment and understanding. Her husband was gone, and she learned that the movie of The Big Wave was never to be distributed or shown in theaters, but she was not discouraged. Now 70 years old, she felt that her life's work was barely begun. There were still children to raise, philanthropic projects to pursue, and more books to write. Buck moved into a smaller New York apartment and prepared for the next stage of her life.

Buck maintained a full schedule of literary and humanitarian activities throughout the last 10 years of her life.

EIGHT

A Legacy of Love

Pearl Buck's adventures continued throughout the last decade of her life. In 1964 she took a trip to India with Danielewski to make another film, *The Guide*. This movie was released and did well, and she took great pride in having participated in a profitable movie venture. During this year she also wrote *A Bridge for Passing* with an account of the filming of *The Big Wave* as a backdrop for her reflections on the loss of her husband. This book had enormous appeal for the American public because of its compassionate description of grief, widowhood, and the end of a long and happy marriage.

Buck next started work on a new novel, *The Living Reed*, about Korea. She had been inspired to write it several years earlier, after having dinner at

the White House with President and Mrs. John F. Kennedy. The president had asked Buck what she thought America should do about Korea, then embroiled in a civil war, and she had promised to write about it and to send Kennedy the first copy of the book. But Kennedy had been assassinated in 1963, even before Buck started writing it.

Buck now returned to an endeavor that she had started several years before: establishing an agency to assist Amerasian children living in poverty in their native lands. She knew that the immigration laws prevented her from bringing these children into the country, and her previous efforts to find a way around the laws had been fruitless. So instead of an adoption agency,

After a visit to President Kennedy in the White House, Buck (front row, third from left) decided to write The Living Reed, *a book about Korea.*

she decided to set up a foundation that would provide money, food, clothing, education, and vocational training to Amerasian children within their own countries. Americans could sponsor an Amerasian child by sending monthly payments to the child through the foundation. Sponsors would receive frequent letters from the child, translated by the foundation staff.

Buck, who firmly believed in independence and self-sufficiency, was de-lighted with her new plan. But she had no knowledge of how to raise funds for her venture. She found the solution in the person of a young dance instructor. Buck had decided that she wanted to learn how to dance, and a call to the Arthur Murray Studio had brought Theodore Harris to her door.

Harris claimed to be an expert fund-raiser, so Buck put him in charge of organizing the Pearl S. Buck Foundation. He sent Buck on a cross-country tour featuring lavish balls, parties, and

The Pearl S. Buck Foundation provides education and support to Amerasian children in their respective homelands.

speaking engagements. Soon the new foundation had the support of well-known people all over the world, including President Eisenhower, Robert Kennedy, and Princess Grace of Monaco. Money poured in, and the foundation moved into a spacious house in Philadelphia.

Buck received three honorary college degrees at this time and published two very successful books, *The Kennedy Women* and *Pearl S. Buck's Oriental Cookbook*. In the Gallup Poll of 1966, she was named one of the 10 most admired American women.

Buck donated her estate, Green Hills Farm, to the foundation. In 1968, she wrote *The New Year*, the story of a child of mixed parentage, and *The Three Daughters of Madame Liang*, a novel telling the story of three young women, each of whom symbolized one way of life in the "new" China. The novel was a Book-of-the-Month Club selection and sold very well. Buck's name continued to appear frequently

Theodore Harris helped Buck raise funds for the Pearl S. Buck Foundation. Their efforts brought the problem of homeless Amerasian children to the attention of many influential people.

in the news, and her books were more widely read than ever before. The foundation was flourishing, providing help to Amerasian children in Korea, Japan, Thailand, Taiwan, and the Philippines.

Then, on a trip through Vermont, Buck passed a small town called Danby and noticed that it was practically a ghost town. Most of the buildings were badly in need of repair. She learned that all the town's young people had left to find jobs elsewhere.

Buck had an idea: She would buy several hundred acres of land and most of the town's buildings and turn the town into a cultural center like Williamsburg, Virginia, and Old Sturbridge, Massachusetts. The project would provide jobs for local residents and the village would prosper once more.

Soon, the buildings of Danby sparkled with fresh white paint and red trim. There was a thriving antique center, a youth center, a country store, and a sandwich shop called the Maple Skillet. Buck and her staff lived in a charming house that she had remodeled, and thousands of tourists flocked to the historic village. Sometimes visitors would catch a glimpse of the writer and humanitarian sitting on the balcony outside her bedroom, her snow-white hair piled high on her head. Buck occasionally autographed her books in the country store and talked for hours with the people who came to visit the village.

By 1968, Pearl Buck's books had been translated and published in 66 countries, and she was America's most widely read author. In 1972, she wrote a magazine article in which she said, "I have begun to live in the 80th year of my life. I do not know where life begins, if indeed there is a beginning, and I do not know when it ends, if indeed there is an end.... I am on my way somewhere, just as I was on the day of my birth."

But that year Buck's health began to fail. Her family, which included fourteen grandchildren, gave her a huge birthday celebration at Green Hills Farm, and in her 81st year she appeared on the *Good Housekeeping* list of most admired women, in third place after Rose Kennedy and Mamie Eisenhower. Her foundation was active in six countries, Welcome House was prospering, and she was at work on another novel. But finally, her strength failed her, and on March 6, 1973, she

Until her death in 1973, Buck continued to receive recognition for her philanthropic and literary achievements.

Buck's last works included the children's book Matthew, Mark, Luke, and John, *which Buck hoped would awaken the world to the poverty and discrimination suffered by Amerasian children.*

Buck walks with three of her grandchildren on the grounds of her Pennsylvania farmhouse, which she eventually donated to the Pearl S. Buck Foundation.

Buck's dedication to humanitarianism reflected her belief that "the uncommitted life is not worth living; we either believe in something, or we don't."

After Buck's death in 1973, the U.S. Postal Service commemorated her life of achievement with a special postage stamp.

died peacefully in her house in Danby. She was buried at Green Hills Farm, which has since become the headquarters of the Pearl S. Buck Foundation. The foundation, Buck's legacy of love, continues her work.

In 80 years, Pearl Buck wrote nearly 100 books, she founded an adoption agency for American children of mixed heritage and a foundation to help Amerasian children in their homelands, and she raised 9 adopted children. Her efforts paved the way for the civil rights leaders of the 1950s and 1960s. She helped remove the stigma from mental retardation and contributed money toward research into its causes. She also expressed women's needs for greater freedom and the

difficulties they faced when trying to pursue successful careers.

Pearl S. Buck, a woman of two careers and two continents, dreamed many dreams and worked tirelessly to fulfill them. In the middle of her long and productive life, she had written a letter to her sister, in which she said, "I do hope I have a long old age, because there are so many things I want to do.... I have at least 20 books I want to write... and I want to enjoy every moment of the children and the world, and beauty, and home besides."

She did all that—and more.

FURTHER READING

Buck, Pearl S. *A Bridge for Passing*. New York: John Day, 1961.

———. *The Good Earth*. New York: John Day, 1931.

———. *My Several Worlds: A Personal Record*. New York: John Day, 1954.

Buck, Pearl S., with Theodore F. Harris. *For Spacious Skies: Journey in Dialogue*. New York: John Day, 1966.

Harris, Theodore F., with Pearl S. Buck. *Pearl S. Buck: A Biography*. New York: John Day, 1963.

Spencer, Cornelia [Grace Sydenstricker]. *Exile's Daughter, A Biography of Pearl S. Buck*. New York: Coward-McCann, 1944.

Stirling, Nora. *Pearl S. Buck: A Woman in Conflict*. Piscataway, NJ: New Century Publishers, 1983.

CHRONOLOGY

June 26, 1892	Born in West Virginia; moves to China three months later
1901	First trip to United States
1911–1914	Second trip to the United States; attends Randolph-Macon College
1917	Marries Lossing Buck in Nanking, China
1921	Carol Buck is born
1931	Publishes *The Good Earth*, her second novel
1932	Awarded the Pulitzer Prize in fiction
1935	Divorces Lossing Buck; marries Richard Walsh
1936	Elected member of the National Institute of Arts and Letters
1938	Receives the Nobel Prize in literature
1966	Dedication of the Pearl S. Buck Foundation for Amerasian Children
March 6, 1973	Dies in Danby, Vermont

INDEX

INDEX

PICTURE CREDITS

Ann La Farge, a graduate of Radcliffe College and Columbia University, has taught in public and private schools and is currently an editor in New York City. She divides her time between Millbrook, New York, and New York City, where she lives with her four children.

Matina S. Horner is president of Radcliffe College and associate professor of psychology and social relations at Harvard University. She is best known for her studies of women's motivation, achievement, and personality development. Dr. Horner serves on several national boards and advisory councils, including those of the National Science Foundation, Time Inc., and the Women's Research and Education Institute. She earned her B. A. from Bryn Mawr College and Ph.D. from the University of Michigan, and holds honorary degrees from many colleges and universities, including Mount Holyoke, Smith, Tufts, and the University of Pennsylvania.

```
B           La Farge, Ann.
Buck
L           Pearl Buck.
```

DATE			

BAKER & TAYLOR